FOR JACK AND JESSICA,
WITH THANKS TO KENDRA AND DAVE

YELLOWSTONE
MORAN

Painting the American West

★ BY ★

LITA JUDGE

VIKING

TOM MORAN had dreams as big as the Montana sky.
He stood in a camp in the the heart of the Rocky Mountains, waiting
nervously. Though Tom knew the men in the camp were scientists, they
looked more like bandits. They eyed him suspiciously. He worried he must
look like a greenhorn, but he wasn't about to admit that he had never
ridden a horse, never shot a gun, and never slept in the open air. Tom
had just traveled two thousand miles to join this expedition
into the land called the Yellowstone. He had to convince
the team's leader, Dr. Hayden, to let him join them.

When Dr. Hayden approached him, Tom could hardly
breathe as he handed the famous geologist a letter.

A few weeks earlier in Philadelphia, Tom had been drawing illustrations of the Wild West for a magazine story. He dreamed of being a great artist and of painting landscapes of places most people had never seen. When his boss told him the government was sending Dr. Hayden and a group of scientists to explore the vast wilderness around the source of the Yellowstone River, he knew he had to join that expedition. Tom was tired of drawing other men's adventures. He was ready to have his own.

Tom wrote to Dr. Hayden, but his letters went unanswered. In June of 1871, he heard that the team of scientists was headed to Fort Ellis, an army outpost in Montana Territory. He decided to ask the army to help him. A general in Philadelphia wrote Tom a letter of introduction and told him he could still catch up with Hayden. Tom packed a carpetbag full of paper, brushes, and paints and raced across the country.

In the camp, Hayden handed the letter back to Tom. "If you're going to join us, we'd best find you a horse." His voice was gruff, but he smiled warmly. "Get yourself outfitted—we leave at sunup tomorrow."

"You're awful skinny," the cook grumbled as Tom gathered his gear together. "Are you ready for mountain passes so steep a man could fall off and disappear? Wild animals? Maybe even Indian attacks?"

Tom didn't answer. He knew he'd fight through almost anything to make it to the Yellowstone. But all afternoon he couldn't get the horse they gave him to budge. Hayden frowned. The Indians called Hayden Man-Who-Picks-Up-Stones-Running, and he wasn't about to wait for a city slicker who didn't know how to handle a horse.

They set out the next morning, and Tom learned to ride quickly. But by noon he was so sore from bouncing on the hard saddle, he had to put a pillow under him. Everyone laughed, but Tom didn't mind the teasing. It was the first of July and he was on his way to the Yellowstone at last.

The group finally stopped and made camp for the night. Lying on the hard ground, Tom thought about the land called the Yellowstone. Few men had explored this high wilderness. Those who had been there told strange tales of mud volcanoes and spouting geysers at a place called Firehole Basin. Tom had even heard of a canyon as deep as a mountain is high. He closed his eyes and wondered, *Could these stories really be true?*

Tom soon began riding beside Will Jackson, the team's photographer. They got to talking about cameras and art. Will was impressed with how much Tom knew.

"With my photographs and your paintings, we could make a good team," Will said. Tom smiled, glad to find a friend.

Often, the team gained only a few miles a day. Days became weeks and the trail disappeared as they pushed farther into the mountains. Tom struggled with his horse. He was tired, dirty, and sore, but he knew they were getting close when they reached the Gardner, a foaming branch of the Yellowstone River.

On July twenty-first, as the team climbed a steep hill, they found themselves entering a strange land.

Tom squinted at blinding white terraces that looked like giant frozen steps of ice leading up the mountainside. These steps held cauldrons of boiling water from underground hot springs. Steam heavy with the rotten-egg stink of sulfur filled Tom's lungs.

They stayed here for three days taking temperature readings and studying the mineral deposits in the hot springs. Tom drew wildly, blinking from the sweat and the stink. Hayden's men admired how hard Tom worked and the way he captured the wild and weird beauty of this place with pencil and watercolor washes.

When the team left the hot springs, they followed a cascading creek. Towering rocks stood like guards, while the water dashed past them and plunged down a steep cliff. This creek would lead them to the Yellowstone River.

After many days of travel, Tom heard the thunder of a waterfall ahead. He rushed through lodgepole pines toward the sound.

Gardiner River
July 1871

pools

pools

mud crater
'Liberty Cap'

exposed surfaces of pinnacles
ore purple / other parts yellow
sulfur

Tower Creek 1871

In the night our horses stampeded twice getting frightened at something. The men succeeded in getting them back. They must have been scared by a bear.

There before him, the river crashed over a
massive rock face, filling the chasm below with
spray that caught rainbows in the sunlight. The stories
were true—they had found the legendary canyon!

Tom couldn't believe what he saw. Even seasoned
explorers like Dr. Hayden gazed with awe at the massive
falls and the thousand-foot-deep gorge. Tom sketched
from the canyon rim, but to paint the falls from every
angle he had to get to the bottom of the ravine.

Hayden and his team were ready to leave the canyon, hoping that if they traveled along its rim, they'd find the source of the Yellowstone River. Most of the men thought Tom would be crazy to try climbing down the perilous ravine. But Will agreed to stay behind and explore the gorge with Tom. Carrying their paint and camera gear, the two men spent hours crawling and sliding down steep rock walls. Bruised and scraped from their trip down, at last they reached the canyon floor.

The falls roared and Tom roared back, his voice joining the powerful crash of the water. He spent hours sketching and memorizing every detail for the huge painting he could already see in his mind.

green   burnt sienna

grey
yellow

yellow

Crystal Falls   1871

Tom hated to leave the canyon, but after a few
days, he and Will had to hurry upriver to meet
Hayden.

The team was camped on the shore of Yellowstone
Lake, the source of the river. The men were happy
to see Tom and Will. That night they sat up late and
shared stories of what they'd seen, and Tom showed
the men his sketches. Even the cook and the others
who had once teased Tom now admired him.

"Once people see your paintings, every expedition
leader in America will want you on their team,"
Hayden told Tom. "But I hope you'll join me again."

After a few days of exploring the lake, Tom
knew he had one last scene to sketch, and that meant
finding the fabled geysers at Firehole Basin. Tom and Will
set out with a small group of men while the rest of the team kept working at
the lake.

This would be the hardest part of the trip. Forest fires often swept through the
Yellowstone. Hard winds blew the dead trees down, leaving a tangle of crisscrossed
logs that were nearly impossible to get through. The men pushed on for thirty miles.
They were low on supplies and some wanted to give up.

Long after dark, sore tired and hungry, they reached the Firehole River. The earth smelled like it was being torn open to its sulfur depths. Tom tried to sleep, but steam filled the night air as geysers erupted. He shivered, and his blanket turned to ice.

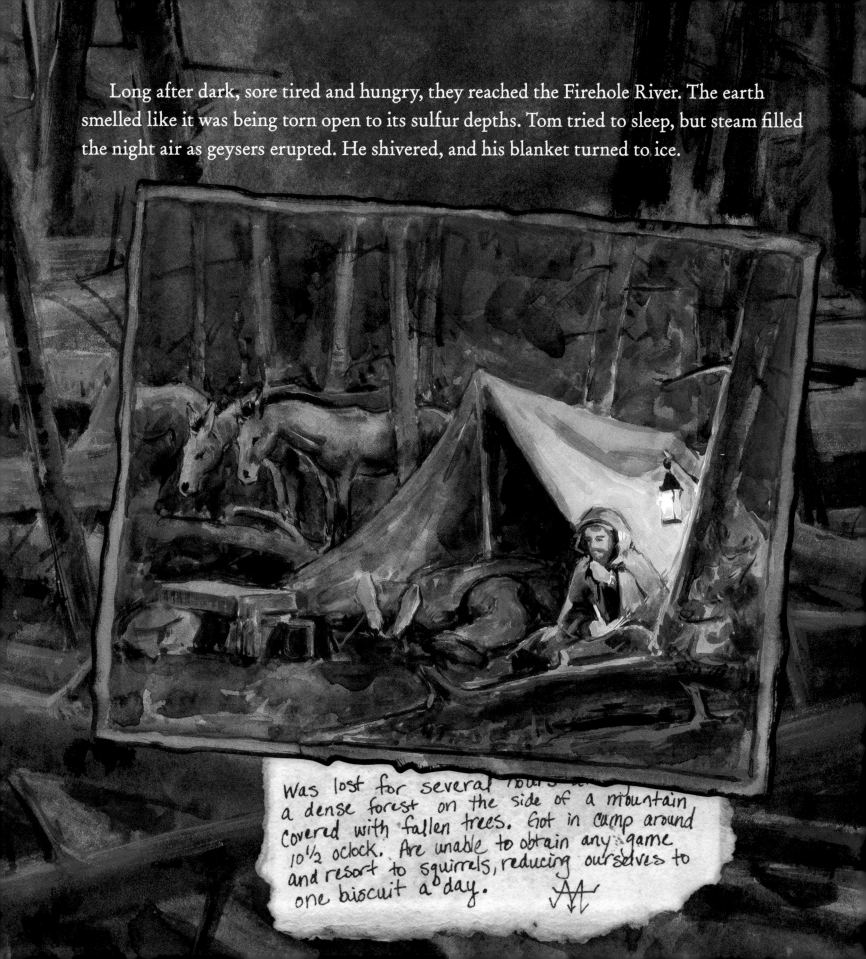

Was lost for several hours in a dense forest on the side of a mountain covered with fallen trees. Got in camp around 10½ oclock. Are unable to obtain any game and resort to squirrels, reducing ourselves to one biscuit a day.

In the morning, Tom woke to finally see Firehole Basin. Fields of sulfur shone pure yellow. Clear, blue-green pools seemed to reach down to the center of the earth. Mud cauldrons burped and sputtered. Geysers hissed and shot jets of boiling water high into the air. When one blew, Tom had to run like crazy to escape the scalding steam.

He learned to listen for the underground rumble just before a geyser erupted. Then he waited, paint and brush ready. No one had painted *this* before!

Meanwhile, Hayden's men recorded water temperatures and timed the eruptions of the geysers. Some blew at regular intervals, and one was so predictable, they called it Old Faithful.

On their last night at Firehole Basin, the moon cast
an eerie light through the steaming geysers.
"I wish all Americans could see this," Tom said.
Will agreed. "Someday, I hope they will."

Tom couldn't wait to get home and paint what he'd seen. When he returned east, he began working on the huge oil painting he had imagined of the legendary canyon. The painting was fourteen feet wide and seven feet tall. Even before it was finished, crowds of people lined up to see it.

That winter, Hayden presented Tom's sketches and smaller paintings to Congress

Thomas Moran, *The Grand Canyon of the Yellowstone*, 1872, the U.S. Department of the Interior Museum, Washington D. C.

and the president, asking them to protect Yellowstone so that it would never be destroyed by the mining and development that were sweeping the west. On March 1, 1872, President Grant signed a bill making Yellowstone America's first National Park.

Tom's dream of painting landscapes of places most people had never seen had come true, but he had never imagined how his paintings would change the course of history.

AUTHOR'S NOTE:

AFTER THE 1871 EXPEDITION, the leaders of every western expedition begged Tom "Yellowstone" Moran to join their teams. He went on to paint in twelve places that became national parks or monuments, including Zion, Yosemite, and Arizona's Grand Canyon. Today, the most massive mountain rising over the valley floor of Teton National Park in Wyoming bears his name: Mount Moran.

I have wanted to create a book about Thomas Moran ever since I was a little girl and first saw his paintings. I visited Yellowstone with my parents every summer and imagined being an explorer and painting a strange and beautiful land few people had ever seen.

Luckily for me, Dr. Hayden encouraged all the men on his team to write journals recording their expedition, and those journals helped me create this book.

We can never know exactly what the men on the expedition said to each other, but I based their dialogue in this story on the letters and journals they wrote. Tom kept a journal, but the other men often wrote more about his experiences than he did. I used Tom's journal and that of a geologist named Albert Peale to create the journals you see in my artwork.

The journals reveal how Tom began the trip as an unprepared young man from the city and grew into an experienced explorer. Though the men really did tease him for using a pillow on his saddle, they all admired his artwork.

Tom's painting *The Grand Canyon of the Yellowstone* appears on the previous pages of this book. The original now hangs in the U.S. Department of the Interior Museum in Washington, D.C. The field sketches throughout these pages are my own paintings, created to look like Tom's. You can see all the places he painted if you visit Yellowstone National Park, where his sketches are preserved at the Mammoth Hot Springs Visitor Center.

ACKNOWLEDGMENTS

I WANT TO THANK my parents, Dale and Elva Paulson, whose passion for the Yellowstone region inspired my own, and who provided some of the photos I used in creating these illustrations.

I also wish to thank H. A. Moore for generously giving me the use of his horse and pack mule so I could gather reference material and retrace Moran's footsteps in Yellowstone for the illustrations in this book. And thanks to my husband Dave, who is no horseman, but posed as Moran.

BIBLIOGRAPHY

Anderson, Nancy. *Thomas Moran*. Washington D.C. and New Haven: National Gallery of Art and Yale University Press, 1997.

Blair, Bob. *William Henry Jackson: The Pioneer Photographer*. Santa Fe: Museum of New Mexico Press, 2005.

Hayden, Ferdinand. *The Yellowstone National Park and the Mountain Regions of Portions of Idaho, Nevada, Colorado and Utah*. Boston: L. Prang and Co., 1876. Reprint, Tulsa, Oklahoma: Thomas Gilcrease Museum Association, 1997.

Merrill, Marlene, editor. *Yellowstone and the Great West: Journals, Letters, and Images from the 1871 Hayden Expedition*. Lincoln: University of Nebraska Press, 1999.

Merrill, Marlene, editor. *Seeing Yellowstone in 1871: Earliest Descriptions and Images from the Field*. Lincoln: University of Nebraska Press, 2005.

Wilkins, Thurman, with Caroline Lawson Hinkley. *Thomas Moran: Artist of the Mountains*. 2nd edition, revised and enlarged. Norman: University of Oklahoma Press, 1998.

U.S. National Park Service, Yellowstone National Park. Moran diary, drawings, and sketches of Yellowstone, summer 1871.

VIKING

Published by Penguin Group

Penguin Young Readers Group, 345 Hudson Street, New York, New York 10014, U.S.A.

Penguin Group (Canada), 90 Eglinton Avenue East, Suite 700, Toronto, Ontario, Canada M4P 2Y3 (a division of Pearson Penguin Canada Inc.)

Penguin Books Ltd, Registered Offices: 80 Strand, London WC2R 0RL, England

First published in 2009 by Viking, a division of Penguin Young Readers Group

1 3 5 7 9 10 8 6 4 2

LIBRARY OF CONGRESS CATALOGING-IN-PUBLICATION DATA

Judge, Lita.

Yellowstone Moran : painting the American West / by Lita Judge.

p. cm.

Includes bibliographical references.

ISBN 978-0-670-01132-2 (hardcover)

1. Moran, Thomas, 1837–1926—Juvenile literature. 2. Moran, Thomas, 1837–1926—Travel—Yellowstone National Park—Juvenile literature. 3. Artists—United States—Biography—Juvenile literature. 4. Painters—United States—Biography—Juvenile literature. 5. Painters—West (U.S.)—Biography—Juvenile literature. 6. Yellowstone National Park—Description and travel—Juvenile literature. 7. Yellowstone National Park—In art—Juvenile literature. 8. West (U.S.)—In art—Juvenile literature. I. Title.

N6537.M6443J83 2009   759.13—dc22   [B]   2008049879

Set in Old Claude   Book design by Nancy Brennan

White Mt.
Hot Springs

Liberty Cap △

Trail from

Gibbons Fork

Madison River

Trail to Virginia City

Nez Perce Creek

Dragon's
Hot

East Fork Firehole River

Great Divide Between Pacific and Atlantic Waters

Lower
Geyser
Basin   ‼△

Excelsior Geyser

Firehole
Basin

Upper
Geyser
Basin

Grotto Geyser △

Castle Geyser △

Old Faithful △
Geyser

Shoshone Lake